MADE IN GOD'S IMAGE SERIES

Book 2

YOU ARE BORN TO WIN

C. Orville McLeish

Made in God's Image Series | Book 2. Copyright © 2019. C. Orville McLeish

All rights reserved. No portion of this book may be reproduced, stored in a retrieval system, or transmitted in any form or by any means – electronic, mechanical, photocopy, recording, scanning, or other – except for a brief quotation in critical reviews or articles, without the prior written permission of the publisher or author.

Published by:

www.hcpbookpublishing.com

ISBN: 978-1-949343-39-7 (paperback)
ISBN: 978-1-949343-40-3 (eBook)

ENDORSEMENTS

This book is profound – the depth of revelation is eye-opening and thought provoking, which is good. It's easy to read, no religious jargons or big fancy words, just straight to the point in a simple and uncomplex language. Points are clear. The only negative for me is that it left me on a high, and I wanted more, so now I have to go dig deeper in the Word. I look forward to future books in this series.

Jovan Walker
Chef, Minister in Training

Interesting read. First chapter was very graphic --- I liked it. The remaining chapters, I would describe as true 'religious hard talk.' It is an in-your-face reality of what's really happening.

Sue-Ann Johnson
Teacher

I dedicate this book to every ONE who was born. You are the 'One.'

TABLE OF CONTENTS

Only One Wins	9
Introduction	23
Chapter One: Your Greatest Enemy	29
Chapter Two: Never Give Up	39
Chapter Three: Human Potential	45
Chapter Four: Access to Divinity	53
Conclusion	59
Connect With Me	63

ONLY ONE WINS

Gamytas is a world on the edge of creation itself. It is the dimension of souls located somewhere beyond space, and outside of time and home to 1.1 trillion life forms, none of whom were meant to stay there. How do I know all of this? We are born knowing. It is our birthright. Who are we? We are the Many and we exist to find the One. It is all we know, it is all we yearn for. The One is all there is. For only when we find the One can we find our true selves, our identity. The Many are not given names, not until we complete the Gauntlet. The Many are born knowing this. The Many lie dormant, but when we wake, we face the Gauntlet - a series of challenges, tests and obstacles. Those that fail will be enveloped by the darkness and cease to exist. But for the one that makes it to the Great Beyond, it is said that they will find the One and their true purpose.

Every single one of us is born wanting to find the One. It's all we crave, and all we wish for. None of us even know what it will be, but we do not need to know. It is not easy to explain or to understand what Gamytas is. It is less of a place, and more of a state of consciousness. Gamytas is all things. Light and dark and up and down and hot and cold. It is the Quantum Foam out of which all the Universe is born. But if the Many are sure of anything, it is that Gamytas is *not* our home, and it is not our destiny to remain there.

I couldn't tell how long I had been awake for. Understanding time is difficult for the Many. An hour? A second? Several days? I couldn't explain my mental grasp of these chronological terms. I was surrounded by inky blackness, and yet I could still see. I hung suspended in the middle of it, the darkness churning around me. I looked down at my body. I had no body. My form was ever-changing. Electric blue, like some sort of plasma, it shifted and rippled and danced ethereally, not quite liquid, not quite gas. Then, suddenly, I knew others were coming. I turned around. A great wave was rolling toward me. And then I realized that it wasn't a wave, it was a collective. A great wall of energy comprised of hundreds of millions of me. Of us. The Many. They were all around me.

"One of us," they chanted at me.

"One of us," I found that the words simply *left* me, without conscious thought.

"Which one?" The Many chanted.

"I am 776,998,416," the number sprang from me as if I had been saying it for my whole existence. It was impossible knowledge, unthinkable knowledge. And yet I knew it was true.

"We are awoken," The Many chanted. "The Gauntlet is here."

I turned back around, suspended in the thick black ether. There it was. The inky blackness before us was swirling, like a jet-black maelstrom, opening up a vast tunnel in the darkness. I knew that if we went through it, the Gauntlet would begin. I somehow knew that we all knew it.

Like a great wave, we moved as one, spreading light through the darkness as we moved into the tunnel. We had no knowledge of what awaited us, but we had no fear. We could feel it, the One, and it awaited us. It called to us. And we had to answer. Suddenly, the passage began to narrow, becoming a funnel-like tube. The Many began to straighten out into a single file to accommodate for the space. Suddenly, the tube snapped shut at one end, as if a section of it had suddenly contracted in on itself. Thousands of us were killed in that instant. I sensed it. I felt it. They were crushed against each other and enveloped by the Darkness. I could feel it, too. It was out there, struggling to crush us. I felt a great rush of energy move through my form, a rush that made me feel hectic and frantic. I began to move faster, desperate to escape the crushing oblivion. And then suddenly I had a word for the energy - panic. All around me, others were moving as fast as they could, as eager as I was to escape their fate.

The passageway began to get narrower

and narrower and narrower. I squeezed through a tiny gap that seemed impossible to get through but didn't stop or look back. If I had, I would have seen more of the Many getting trapped in the receding passageway. And then the jaws of the beast snapped shut on them. They were gone. It was dark again. Pitch-black. I couldn't see, and yet I still could. I turned around. More than half of the Many had been killed, and yet none of us stopped or paused to mourn or spare a thought. Our purpose was to continue. We had to. Suddenly, I stopped in my tracks. My instinct. I couldn't explain how, but I knew that there was something waiting, some kind of wall in the darkness. I...*reached out* and felt it. Malleable, but apparently impregnable. Some kind of transparent barrier? The Others had begun to feel it too. They piled up against the barrier, pushing and shoving, attempting to force their way through. The barrier bent under the force but did not break.

They were wrong, I knew. That wasn't the way. Again, I reached out to the barrier and placed my electric-blue body against it. I concentrated and felt the power inside me crackling and bubbling to a boil. Suddenly, I felt the barrier begin to give way, as if it were wilting under the heat from the energy in my form. Yes, definitely wilting. It relaxed and contracted and turned from solid to liquid as it gave way, and then suddenly I had the word for it. The barrier *melted*.

I pushed my way through the perforation left in the barrier and wriggled free. I felt a second wave of rushing inside me, but different from the first time. The first time I had felt panic, this was different. I felt *elation*. I was happy! The Many had noticed what I had done, high above them, and suddenly they swarmed for the hole I had left. They collided into each other as they attempted to force their way through the barrier, and I knew that they would kill each other in the attempt. Sure enough, they began to crush each other, millions of us all desperately trying to get through a tiny gap in the barrier.

I didn't stop to look or stop to help. It was against my nature to help, or to care at all. The Gauntlet was all that mattered. The passage suddenly began to pitch upward. I sensed a beacon of power from above me. I looked and there it was. High above me in the distance, it hung suspended in the darkness, pulsing and ebbing with power. I felt a huge strain on my body, almost like there was some kind of force pulling me downward. It became harder and harder to move as the passageway that I was following pitched higher and higher, until I was moving vertically. I could feel the strain in my very being. I couldn't explain the feeling, but it was bad. It was uncomfortable, it was...*pain*.

I gave it all I had, but I began to slow. Every movement was painful. And then, out of the corner of my eye, I saw a flash of blue. One of us. I hadn't been the only one to make it past the barrier! There were two of us left. Just two, but only One can make it. I was slowing, every movement sending jolts of pain through my body as I struggled to make a vertical ascension, but the Other was moving, strong and powerfully, holding a true course as it moved upward toward the One.

I didn't think, I didn't plan, I simply acted. I threw my body sideways. I do not know what made me do it. I collided right into the Other and he was knocked headlong into the Darkness. I saw it envelope him, saw his bright blue energy signature swallowed whole. He was gone.

I harnessed every last scrap of energy I had left and continued on my course upward. I was twenty feet from the One. Ten feet. Five. As I got closer, I realized that the One was not what I had first thought. It resembled a funny-looking cocoon of some sort. Just as it seemed I was close enough to touch it, the world went dark. Not dark like before, this was real dark. I couldn't see, I couldn't move. I was surrounded, engulfed in some kind of…liquid? I felt heavy. How long had I been here? Where was the One? I was confused.

Slowly, dazedly, I looked down at my body, expecting to see the bluish hue of my plasma-like form. I was wrong. The bluish hue was gone, replaced by something a lot darker, closer to tan. Two fleshy limbs were wrapped around me. I realized with a start that they were *attached* to me. A great feeling of despair welled up inside me. Was this it? Was this the end of the Gauntlet? I had expected to find what the Many yearn for with every fiber of our existence. I had expected to find my purpose, my true name, my true identity. I had hoped to find...*myself*. But this was all there was. A dark abyss?

I became suddenly aware that I had been trapped in the liquid for a lot longer than it seemed. I couldn't say how long. Was this time? Time was difficult. Suddenly, I felt something jerk at my body. I didn't like it. Bright light suddenly began to fill the dark cavern, and then without warning, I felt the liquid draining away. I suddenly heard a terrible sound, and the liquid began to wash me away. Once again, panic welled up inside me. I was being pulled, pulled with force. I struggled, but it was no use. I was being pulled towards the terrible, screeching sound that filled my…ears? With a sudden shock, I realized that I was making the screeching sound. It seemed appropriate. I was experiencing multiple things at the same time. I was in pain, I was distressed, I was confused. Somehow, I knew that that screeching noise was an amalgamation of everything I was feeling.

I heard a strange voice from high above me in the light.

"Darling, it's a boy!"

And then, once again, the world went black.

When I awoke, I felt…different. I was lying on my back, wrapped in something soft, and white. I could *see*. The world around me wasn't dark, wasn't black, and was no abyss. It was a brilliant splash of color, and smells and swirling noise. I couldn't take it all in. I opened my eyes wide and simply…was. There was a face smiling down at me. A face lined with tiredness. I instantly felt a warm rush of affection. I couldn't explain it, but I felt a connection to this face.

"Hello, Oran," the face said warmly.

And with those two words, my mind exploded. Glorious new knowledge flooded into my mind, knowledge that I knew I would not remember when next I awoke. I tried with all my might to speak, to form words, but try as I might, my mouth would not obey me. The One was real. The Great Beyond was real. I was here. I *was* the One. I had thought that my journey was over, but my journey was just beginning. I was no longer one of the Many, I was my own person.

I had wished to know my true name, to know my true self and to know my true destiny. My name is Oran. My name means 'Light.' I am a human being. And my destiny is whatever I make it, and I will make it amazing.

INTRODUCTION

While it was possible to write this book from a doctrinal perspective, replete with Scriptural references, and theological quotes, I intentionally decided not to do that. I believe Scripture is relevant to most of humanity, and everybody reads it, whether they are believers are not. Those who succeed in our world have somehow managed to extract the spiritual principles in the Bible, and apply it successfully to their lives, some without walking the path of indoctrination and church life, and it's all good. Believe it or not, there is a lot of principles that the church can learn from the world. The knowledge about who we are, and humanity's role in creation does not belong to only one set of people; it belongs to everyone. Religion, particularly, Christianity has succeeded in keeping the Bible, and the gospel of Jesus alive and on the lips of men, but we have failed in other areas.

The danger with religion is that we try to encapsulate God in a particular doctrine and belief system, thereby restricting His true nature as God. If we had succeeded as the church to represent God well, Christianity would be more effective in our communities and society at large, because they are already adapting to a lot of the morals and principles that sit at the foundation of life. God doesn't change, as we understand change to be, but He is not restricted by our belief or doctrine either because He is God. Doctrine that may seem relevant today can become obsolete tomorrow and if we fail to let go of the old to embrace the new, we will end up becoming like those who met Jesus with great hostility instead of faith. The church then (Scribes, Pharisees, Teachers of the Law) could not let go of all that was said and done under Moses' regime, and they were quite content with repeating the same pattern over and over again, even when it was obvious that God was moving His people to another dimension, and that is our issue today.

We prefer to teach our children to carry on our same dead practices instead of challenging them to build on the little that we know. We need to stop seeing the world from the perspective of sinner and saint, saved and unsaved, going to heaven and going to hell. For God so loved the 'World' that He 'Gave' heaven's most prized treasure to redeem it. We need to see the world from the perspective of humanity, made in the image and likeness of God, even if that image is presently obscured or distorted. God loves all human beings. The world is a recipient of God's love, not His judgment and the only thing we owe our fellow man is love. Love is the alchemic principle that will give birth to the next generation of humans, who understands who they are and whose they are, and it is from this perspective that I write.

The captioned story "Only One Wins" depicts the journey of a soul from the ethereal dimension to this one. It is a difficult journey filled with obstacles, and millions of participants, but only One can win. All the others die in the race, but only One can come out on top.

That One is given a unique opportunity to change the world into which he or she is born. They are born free from fear, doubt, feelings of inadequacy or self-worth. They are born strong, selfless, fearless, confident, honest and filled with love and faith. They are born to win.

GAMYTAS is the dimensions of soul. It exists outside of time, and the details of its function and reality is still a mystery. Sexual intercourse is one of the most powerful technologies given to humanity because in the process of pleasure, a race is initiated among millions of participants, but only One can win. The GAUNTLET is the process of conception. The MANY are all the potentials. The TUNNEL is where the egg of a woman is located; the ONE is the egg of a woman and ORAN, whose name means 'Light', the One who connects with the ONE, the One who wins, is YOU!

You have the potential to be great, but there are obstacles that you must overcome. However, you should know, that the only one who can stop you from winning in life, is YOU.

CHAPTER ONE

YOUR GREATEST ENEMY

It breaks my heart to see a human being on the streets begging. These sights are very prevalent here in the Caribbean. We see others walking half-naked on the roads, completely out of their minds. My heart aches when I witness two people fighting each other, brandishing stones, knives and guns with an intent to inflict harm without thought, remorse or reservations. I realize by mere observation alone that we are ignorant to our connectiveness to each other, and to the unseen world. We spend so much time fighting each other, or some demon or the other, thinking that they are our greatest enemies, and we cannot progress without defeating them. Yet, our lives don't improve, our stories don't change, and we still fail to make the connection that we are, in fact, ignoring the only one who can truly stand in your way --- and that's you. The greatest enemy you need to defeat in order to step into greatness, and for your true nature to immerge, is yourself.

There is a reason Jesus made the profound statement that you cannot follow in His footsteps, unless you first deny self. The original word use for "deny" in Mark 8:34, Luke 9:23, Matthew 16:24 is *aparneomai* which means to *utterly disown or abstain,* which is a different word and meaning from the "deny" which is used in 2

You Are Born to Win

Timothy 2:13. The English language is very limited, so one word can be used in Scripture multiple times, with multiple meanings, so we have to be careful when studying for meaning. To "deny" self speaks to a radical disconnect from that which would hold us back or confine us to perpetual failure.

As you progress through your life from birth to where you are now, your life's experiences, everything you have witnessed, heard, thought about, accepted, and spoken resulted in self duplication. Yes, I do believe a human being can duplicate himself. So, there are many versions of yourself living in your body, and each version of yourself has a voice. It's not always a demon. A lot of the things you thought the devil made you do was you convincing yourself to do it. Addiction is also a war against a version of yourself created by repeatedly participating in an act and enjoying it. If you are caught in a repetitive cycle of doing something you don't want to do, it simply means there is a version of yourself that likes to do it. This is also why many people seeking deliverance almost always fall back in the same patterns. You cannot cast out a person's "self." Why do you think pastors who consistently abuse little children or rape women, or get involved in extra martial affairs are able to still perform their ministerial duties, sometimes very effectively too, until they are found out? There are many husbands and wives living double and triple lives, who have found a way, by an act of their own will, to keep their separate lives from ever colliding in this life. While this is to their own detriment, people tend to fragment and compartmentalize their different selves, and are able to live multiple lives in one body. Schizophrenia is not really a disease. We are all schizophrenia's, it's just that most of us have it under control.

God said to man, "Be fruitful and multiply…" Adam could not fulfill his responsibility in overseeing creation if he was restricted to one location, with no means of transportation. We always had the potential to "self-multiply" but we didn't start replicating our evil selves until Adam and Eve sinned. Remember, Adam sinned without having a conversation with the devil. Human beings do not make any decision without having a conversation, so who did he talk to? Adam's offspring, Cain, murdered his brother for no apparent reason. Abel had done nothing to him. We read that God spoke with Cain just prior to him carrying out this premediated murder and told him he needed to learn to master sin. Immediately after hearing that from God personally, Cain went out to the field with his brother, and murdered him. There is no record of Cain speaking with a devil, so who convinced him that he had to take the life of his brother? The only person he talked to was God. Here we also see just how powerful the human will is; not even a conversation with God deterred Cain from what he had resolved to do in his heart.

Our many selves can become an adversary to our true identity in God and can hinder our growth and development. In order to move into our greatness, we must overcome our selves and it is not as easy as it sounds. The process is continuous and takes effort. Even the process of salvation seems like a lifelong experience, because it's all about bringing the many into one.

So, how do we defeat our many selves? One of the best ways I have found is through knowledge, faith and declaration. We must study who God says we are, commit it to memory or write it down and speak it every day. We must allow, intentionally, all our decisions to be made based on our growing knowledge about who we are, and Who we belong to. If we practice this every day, the other voices become irrelevant, and eventually start to disappear. It takes work, and it takes effort. So, the Bible now says, "let God be true, but every man a liar; as it is written (about you).." (Romans 3:4). Do you realize that Jesus also used the phrase, "It is written…"? All that is written either reminds us of who we really are, or it reminds us of who God is, and who we are in Him. This knowledge must sit at the very foundation of our beings, and you don't have to be a believer in Jesus to benefit from these spiritual principles. Sometimes I think the world understands who they are as human beings better than believers do because they practice meditation and affirmations, and we don't.

It is time we shake ourselves free from the shackles of ignorance and realize that we are not insignificant and worthless. We were made in the image and likeness of God, and that must mean something. All the different versions of yourself that you have allowed to come into existence can only be dealt with by you. No one can destroy and render them impotent but you. In the process of working out your own "salvation," you need to be intentional and deliberate in your approach, but above all, don't ever give up trying. Your will is extremely powerful, and it is one of those attributes that make you more like God than anything else. Refuse, by an act of your will, to be anyone else, but who God says you are, and the many will begin to conform to the one.

CHAPTER TWO

NEVER GIVE UP

Life is a race and every 'One' can win. There are enough resources in this world for every 'One' to have more than enough. It took me many years and trudging through many treacherous waters to understand the knowledge I am sharing with you in this book. I desire to save you some time so your process, and the emergence of your true self can be fast-tracked. It is a grueling journey, and you need to make this your mantra, "Never give up."

When the storms of life come, and they will; when trauma hits close to home; when everything you try has failed, don't give up. When your dreams turn to nightmares; and all your friends vacate your life, and family turn against you, never give up. When the unforeseen and unexpected happen, and you are thrust into an experience you never ask for, or think you can't survive, never give up. It may not look like it now, but everything you experience in life will become relevant at some point in your journey to success because it is working for your good, somehow. So, never give up.

One of the perks of getting older is that you get to look back at all your mistakes with clarity. Yes, I have many regrets, but if I had made different choices then, I would not be where I am now. I realize that the past is only a reference point, and all that matters is NOW and the decisions we make going forward.

Life is a journey, and we have different and unique destinations. There will be some commonality, but the journey to get where we need to go will look different for each of us. I see the statistics; I know people are hurting, struggling, traumatized, and suffering on all levels, but I believe there is a light in each of us waiting to break forth, and no one will be called upon to make the greatest contribution to that but you. You must be willing to participate in your own emergence, in your own coming forth, for if you ever decide to give up, and stop trying, no one can stop you from walking away.

Take charge of your life and realize that you are in control. You decide your fate; you decide your responses to what is happening around you. You decide what you think about, and what you speak from your mouth. But in understanding these attributes about yourself, you must also assume the responsibility that comes with it, because the world you create today will be the reality for your children tomorrow. If I teach my nieces and nephews anything, it is to never give up and never be deterred by obstacles in their way. I encourage them to always press forward, and use their will to push, and not relent and take a seat on the bench when things get rough, or it doesn't go as expected.

Creation awaits your decision to be a participant, and not just a mere spectator. You have a part to play in life; and that is why you are here. There is no substitute for you. The world will either get what you carry, or you take it back with you when you leave. You carry something that this world needs, and you must never give up until it emerges, and takes root. Don't allow the seeds of greatness planted within your being to die with you. Don't die until you have fulfilled your calling.

Aim high, dream big and never give up. You were born to win. If this wasn't true, you would not be here. Only winners are born because the journey from conception to birth is a treacherous one, and there are a million things that could have hindered you from being here, but nothing stopped you. There is nothing that should stop you now from achieving your dreams, no matter how impossible it may seem.

CHAPTER THREE

HUMAN POTENTIAL

All human beings possess greatness. We all have the potential to be a far greater version than ourselves. Most will live out their entire lifetimes and not even scratch the surface of what they have the potential to do and accomplish on this earth, but you don't have to be counted among them.

In our quest to be greater, we must also be cautious. Each of us have the propensity for both evil or good. We can be great from the perspective of evil, or we can be great from the perspective of good. From a Biblical standpoint, Adam was created perfect and predominantly good, yet he had the potential to choose evil. If he didn't, it would have been impossible for him to make the choice he did. The knowledge of good and evil is a tree available to every man.

Greatness can also be achieved by virtue of good that is not godly, God-centered or Christ-centered. We can achieve great things without faith in God. As a matter of fact, a careful reading of Scripture will tell us that we only need to "believe" in order to achieve. It didn't say "believe in God." If more than one human being can come together in unity of mind, language and desire, they can achieve the impossible, as demonstrated at the Tower of Babel. History confirms that we can be great individually, and even greater collectively, without faith in God.

My issue is, if a man can achieve some of the things we have heard about and seen in our history; building airplanes, skyscrapers, amassing more wealth than his entire generation can spend in a lifetime, and do all this without surrendering their lives to Christ, then what can those who believe in Jesus actually accomplish? I believe the church has failed miserably in tapping into this reality because of fear, uncertainty and ignorance. We never stopped to think that if a witch can fly, then it means a human being can fly. If a magician can create an illusion, then it means a human being can create an illusion. If a man can walk through walls, and walk on water, then it simply means a human being can do that. The church flipped the script on Truth by declaring demons to be more powerful than human beings, yet humans are those believed to be created in the image and likeness of God, not angels or demons. What blows me away is just how significantly powerless the man who has no idea who he is can become.

We are so great, and so powerful that the Bible says we can manifest anything by mere thought and speech. I think we all should personally make it a goal to explore this reality in detail from a scientific, religious, emotional, psychological and social perspective. We should examine what makes agreement between human beings so powerful. Just how connected are we from the ethereal realm?

We can't look at life and our makeup without admitting that there is a vast world beyond this one. Too many of us live out our lives without looking up in the sky at nights. One glance into a starry night should confirm that there must be more to our existence than living a mediocre, unfulfilled life; being underpaid and overworked. Someone out there has a better plan for our lives. We need to request to see the blueprint we were made from, because there is far too much about us that we don't know. Surely, we don't still hold on to the fact that all this came out of nothing, and if creation did have a Creator, isn't it worth looking into? What would such a Being desire of us? If He made us, why did He and for what reason? What purpose do we serve? What is our role in creation? How connected are we to nature, and all living things? Who are we really?

One of the things that blocks us, I believe, from emerging as our true self, in God, is our freedom to choose. Human will is a powerful force, and there is no power in the universe that can tame it. Your will is your true power. You get to choose what you believe, and only you can change your own theology and doctrine about life, existence, human potential, and God. I only ask that you observe life, and yourself with an open mind, and seek out knowledge, because it is there. It sits in the open, waiting for you to receive it.

History confirms that you don't need to accept Jesus as your Lord and Saviour to achieve great things and open the door for all your desires to be granted. Hard work, persistence and wisdom can get you there. But I believe you can achieve far greater things with Jesus. Christians have been a poor example of this, but it doesn't mean it's not true.

Fact is, you have a lot of potential with or without faith in Jesus Christ. But I believe that in Christ, we are closer to our original temperament as a man made in the image and likeness of God.

CHAPTER FOUR

ACCESS TO DIVINITY

In the beginning….God made man in His own image, and likeness. If we can forget everything we know, and just think about that one statement, I think we will have a better understanding about who man is. All the controversy, doctrinal debates, and theological conflicts is irrelevant, because the only thing that really matters is seeing life and existence through the eyes of God. After all, He made it all, and He has a purpose for everything He made.

You have a choice, and no one can take that away from you. You can go ahead and seek after life, and everything it has to offer, and you may even find some measure of success without even believing that there is a God. But, if you are willing to consider the possibility that there is a Creator, and the Bible is true, then this Chapter is specifically for you.

God made all things, including human beings. He made everything with a purpose and equips everything, so it is possible for what was created to carry out the purpose for which it was created. Human beings were given the mandate to take charge of the earth (rule and take dominion). Even today, we find that God rarely, directly intervenes in the affairs of man, so our children are raped and murdered, crime continues to escalate, economies crash, and wars emerge. The church helps very little with a majority of us thinking that prayer is about repetitively asking God to come and fix the broken world, when it is clear from Scripture that we were given the responsibility, and the tools to do the fixing. You have the Holy Spirit, the same Spirit who hovered over chaos and brought order in the beginning of time. He lives inside your physical body, as a believer. You have faith that can move a physical mountain, because every man is given a measure of faith. You have love that can transform worlds, because the love of God is shed abroad in your heart. You lack nothing. You have everything you need for life, and godliness. So, stop wasting time asking God to do things He already asked you, and created you to do. God is looking for partners, not puppets. Real prayer is engaging God at a certain level until He completely saturates your being, so when you walk, He walks; when you talk, He talks.

God has given human beings access to divinity. We can share in the same nature that Jesus Christ has. He gave us the keys and told us to go change the world. He allowed the physical temple to be destroyed in 70A.D., after the veil that separated humanity from the presence of God was torn in two, giving humanity access once again to the throne of God. It was God's idea to make you like Him, so why do you reject His offer, and call it humility?

You have what you need to be great and do extraordinary exploits. You have what you need to win. You have access to the greatest power-source in all existence and you need to understand

You Are Born to Win

what this means for you. A powerless believer is one who is standing in front of a huge sapphire door that opens up into an eternity of unlimited possibilities, holding the key to the door in their hand, and thinking they can't get in. I believe God's answer to most Christians prayer today is a simple, "Come in." But we prefer to stay outside the door, shouting at God, and skipping around like crazy people, producing nothing that will change and make the earth better.

You carry an unlimited supply of resources, concepts for new inventions, business ideas, wealth-building talents and abilities. You have access to an eternity of knowledge, and power that transcends time, space and matter. God, the awesome Deity, whose very presence provokes fear because the fabric of His being is said to be "Unapproachable light" has given us all an invitation to come to Him, to know Him and to partner with Him in establishing a new heaven and a new earth. Jesus Christ is the door. You need to ask, "Door to what?" By Him, you have access and access is all you need to win in life.

CONCLUSION

I have come to accept that the blessings of God and His promises are real, but they are not magic. Jesus says His Father works, and He works. So, in the grand scheme of creation, the Father is "doing." It is unfair of us to sit down and keep expecting our blessings to be delivered to us on a silver platter. We want God to fix the world, fix our lives, fix our finances with a snap of His fingers. While I believe He can, because nothing is impossible for Him; and we can sit passive and be blessed, because nothing is impossible to him who believes, there is work and effort involved for the most part. Before sin entered this world, Adam and Eve had responsibilities, and they were expected to work. I assume as well that they were given a day of rest, as God rested on the seventh day.

Every blessing God gives is given in seed form, which must be cultivated if we are to experience a harvest. Even Adam and Eve, in their perfect human form, was placed in a garden to cultivate it. One of the original mandates given to man is to "replenish" the earth, which means when resources are running out, we have the responsibility to replenish it. We have made God into a fairy godfather. We want Him to fetch our water, our food, our clothes and give us money we don't work for. We want Him to heal us, while we give scant regard to exercise and eating nourishing foods. We want Him to deliver us from the adversaries of our own making. We don't want to learn how to do anything or be given responsibility for anything or anyone. But that era of humanity is slowly ending.

Those who learn to cultivate the seeds within them, and overcome the adversary of self, will walk in abundance, health and influence. Those who are praying for the great magician to wave his wand and make their lives better will die praying and waiting, and the seeds God has deposited in them will be buried with them in the grave, never to come to fruition or provide a harvest for the generations to follow. Every generation I have known has had to start from scratch and find their own way because nothing was left for them but the parched wilderness of a dead, powerless religion that talks but is incapable of demonstrating what is said in their day to day lives.

This is a personal invitation to you, because I believe that what is inside you is greater than you know now, but it's a seed that will grow with knowledge, hard work, persistence, and integrity. But if you really want to emerge as your greater self without hindrance or restrictions, then you need to come in alignment with Jesus Christ who suffered and died so you can once again be given access to what you had with Him before sin entered into our context. He is the door to an unlimited treasure house, and an eternity of ecstatic bliss. When we partner with Him, all things are possible.

CONNECT WITH ME

Facebook:
authorcorvillemcleish

Instagram:
cleveland.mcleish

Daily Devotional:
www.madeingodsimage.blog

email:
info@hcpbookpublishing.com

Whassap:
1-876-352-2650

www.ingramcontent.com/pod-product-compliance
Lightning Source LLC
Chambersburg PA
CBHW052207110526
44591CB00012B/2116